My Bully

Story by : Nati Carrillo
Illustrated by : Xuyinyin

SKY WILLABEA
-PRESS-

Published 2019

ISBN-13: 978-1-7338402-0-0 (Paperback, 5x8")

ISBN: 978-1-7338402-4-8 (Paperback, 8x10")

ISBN: 978-1-7338402-5-5 (Ebook)

Published by Sky Willabea Press

Problems are like math they all have a solution. It may take some time to find the right answer or help when you need it; just don't give up. We ALL deserve a BULLY FREE ENVIRONMENT. Be the difference. TAKE ACTION and SPEAK UP!

Finding answers:
Stopbullying.gov
Stompoutbullying.org

Is it someone who looks **big, mean, or ugly?**

Or is it someone who is **gentle, timid,** and **snugly?**

Is it someone who holds the **key** to your happiness?

Or is it someone who is **keeping you from it?**

Is it someone who has **control** over you?

And threatens
to hurt you
if you don't do
as he wishes?

Or is it someone that **helps you** do the dishes?

Is it someone that **wakes you up** every morning?

Or is it someone that keeps you up all night?

Is it someone who plays with you?

Or is it someone that **doesn't let you** play?

Is it someone
you **trust**
and
confide in?

Or is it
someone that
shames you
from within?

Whom ever,
your bully turns out to be.
**Speak up,
don't let them win.**
We all have a voice
to let others know,
**That your bully
has to go!**

Please understand fully,

I want you to know,

To rid yourself of your bully,

You have to act and say NO!

About the author:

Nati Carrillo was born in Edcouch, Texas. Married with four children. She is a graduate of the University of Texas at Brownsville with a Master's degree in nursing with a specialty in nursing education. She is a Board Certified Family Nurse Practitioner. She has written three books: Bullies Create Bullies, a fiction/biography geared toward teenagers dealing with bullies, The Slippery Slopes of Consequences, a fiction story of irony and how one mistake no matter how small causes the downfall of the whole Wee family, and Shattered, a dark fiction story about how a young girl's abused life haunts her into her teenage years.

www.ingramcontent.com/pod-product-compliance
Lightning Source LLC
Chambersburg PA
CBHW042105040426
42448CB00002B/146